THE LADYBIRD 'UNDER FIVE' SERIES

Learning
with
Mother

*by ETHEL and
HARRY WINGFIELD*

Publishers: Ladybird Books Ltd . Loughborough
© Ladybird Books Ltd (formerly Wills & Hepworth Ltd) 1972
Printed in England

Weaving Simple paper-weaving is easy and effective, and gives a very satisfying sense of achievement to a child. The result can be a table mat or wall decoration – a personal present from your child to you.

Several sheets of stiff paper or card, each a different colour, are all that will be needed. One of these sheets forms the base. On the reverse side of it, parallel lines should be drawn about $\frac{3}{4}''$ apart (Fig. 1) to within $\frac{3}{4}''$ of the top and bottom. The base should then be folded across the middle and cut along each line from the fold to within $\frac{3}{4}''$ of the edge (Fig. 2) and opened out flat again.

From the other sheets, which must be rather wider than the base, strips can be cut, all $\frac{3}{4}''$ wide (the drawing of guide lines will make this easier). These strips form the weaving material. The strips can be woven into the base, alternatively or in sequence, to form a pattern, each strip being fitted snugly against the previous one (see page opposite).

The ends can be tucked under and secured by strips of Sellotape (Fig. 3).

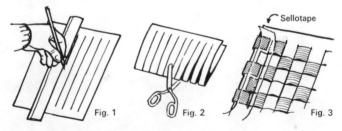

Fig. 1   Fig. 2   Sellotape   Fig. 3

Discuss the picture with your child.

0 7214 0291 7

Indoor Gardening

It is natural for children to be interested in plants which grow and change, developing roots, shoots, buds, flowers and seeds. A child acquires this interest as a matter of course if he or she is fortunate enough to have a garden. If the family has no garden, then mother or father can provide an alternative.

By growing beans and peas in glass jars indoors, the child is provided with a close-up view of one of the miracles of nature. There is a sense of involvement in keeping the seeds damp, and the reward of seeing the day-to-day growth of roots, shoots and leaves.

An oblong of blotting paper can be fitted around the inside of a glass jar, touching the inside all round. The jar should be filled with sand almost to the top of the paper. The peas, beans or other large seeds in each jar should be spaced around between the glass and the paper. The sand must then be thoroughly moistened and kept damp.

The tops of carrots or parsnips can be cut off, placed in a saucer and kept moist. They will very soon sprout new, green life.

Discuss the picture with your child. Ask if he or she knows which is a root and which is a shoot.

carrot

peas

beans

Making a Clock

By the age of five a child is very aware of time and the necessity of keeping to time. Time patterns the daily routine. 'Time to catch the bus', 'Time for tea', and so on. A child will often ask what time of day it is, and has probably enjoyed wearing a toy watch.

Making and using this toy clock will give a lot of pleasure. To make it, all that is needed is a cardboard plate (bought from the stationers), stiff, coloured card for the hands, a paper fastener (the brass fold-over type), and a crayon or felt pen to mark the numbers. When cutting out strips of card for the hands, they can be measured against the plate to obtain the correct length, and then each hand cut to a point at one end. The centre of the plate should be pierced and also the blunt end of the hands. All this will probably be within the capabilities of your child, as will be the numbering. You can help if there is any difficulty. The hands are joined to the clock-face with the paper fastener, which is inserted from the front and folded over at the back, making sure that the hands will rotate without being too loose. A small circle of card, to act as a washer as shown, is helpful.

Talk about the picture. Talk about the things you do throughout the day at fixed times. Interest your child each day by saying what happens at such and such o'clock. Let interest grow naturally – do not *press* your child to learn.

The Child as Discoverer

Discovery begins with curiosity, but a child needs help and encouragement if this natural curiosity is to lead into the process of learning. We need to remind ourselves that a child views with fresh vision and a sense of wonder those miracles of nature and the achievements of man which to us may seem commonplace.

Like the parent in the picture, you may be asked questions such as – "What makes the crane work?" involving some mention of electricity in the answer, or "Why are they lifting the lorry up?" which would lead to a description of the new methods of 'container' transport. There is no need to avoid such subjects or situations. If your own knowledge is not sufficient there are plenty of books which will assist you – many of the Ladybird reference books being ideal for supplying information with which to answer children's questions.

Children not only enjoy story and picture books, they also enjoy those books from which they – and grown-ups – can learn together and which make learning fun. Curiosity, patiently and willingly fostered by a child's parents, becomes a powerful force for learning.

Talk about the picture. Help your child to recall situations which have interested him or her.

Construction Sets

As children grow older, the urge for realism also grows. Their need is for basic play material with which to build. They are impressed and excited by buildings, cranes, bridges, tunnels, and the elaborate engineering structures which they see around them or in books and on television. It may not be the purpose of a child to build working models but rather to achieve the spectacular.

This construction set – plus the natural driving force of a 4 or 5-year-old – enables the spectacular to be achieved. The toy's versatility also encourages the development of imagination and creative ability.

Construction sets similar to the one shown opposite can be obtained from Paul and Marjorie Abbatt Ltd., 94 Wimpole Street, London, W.1., and E. J. Arnold and Sons Ltd., Butterley Street, Leeds; or on enquiry at any good toy shop.

Discuss the picture with your child.

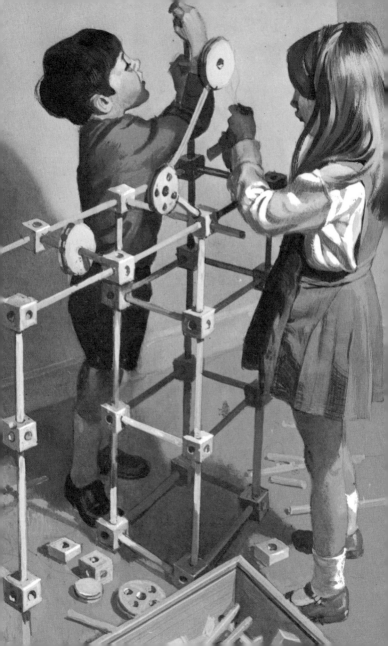

Group Play

Children playing together provide one another with the best possible social experience. They are sharing common interests, the basis of all good relationships. They are developing independence in thought and action, and developing also some degree of conformity so necessary if they are to become good members of society.

Here are some group games which children of four and five years enjoy playing:

Ring a ring of roses. The farmer's in his den. I sent a letter to my love. In and out the windows. Two little blue-birds in the window. Here we come gathering nuts in May. Here we go round the mulberry bush. Jack be nimble. Oranges and lemons. Here's a little man marching – marching round the town. See the little bunny sleeping. Looby Loo. Peter hammers with one hammer. The big ship sails through the Alley, Alley O. Sheep, sheep come over. Hide and Seek.

Information on such group games, music, songs and rhymes for the under-fives can be obtained for a few pence from The Nursery Schools Association of Great Britain and Northern Ireland, 87 Stamford Street, London, S.E.1.

Talk about the picture. Ask your child if he knows how to play any of the games listed above. Ask what particular games appeal to him or her.

Going into Hospital

Every mother knows how disturbing, even frightening, the unfamiliar can be to a young child who has few past experiences on which to draw for reassurance. For instance, to take a child into hospital, away from familiar home surroundings, provokes not only fear of what is going to happen but fear of almost everything else, fear of night-time, of unfamiliar toilets and strange food, unfamiliar clothes and faces, fear of medicine and perhaps of other children. How much better if Mother, on whom a child depends so much, can give the necessary reassurance.

Fortunately the children's departments in our modern hospitals have a very forward-looking attitude to the problem of making a sick child happy and so aiding recovery. The most urgent need of any child – that for its Mother – is met. Mother can be there, to be seen and talked to, to help with meals and toileting, to help with dressing and undressing and to sit in a comfortable armchair and nurse and comfort her child, perhaps while watching a familiar television programme.

A mother can spend the whole day with her child, and in some circumstances the night also. She can bring a brother or sister into the ward. She is not just a visitor for an hour but someone who is sharing the whole experience.

In turn a child can share her with other children in need of comfort and reassurance, so making a stay in hospital a rewarding experience.

Discuss the picture with your child, what the children are doing, which are nurses and which is a mother and so on.

16

The publishers wish to acknowledge the assistance of The Good Hope Hospital, Sutton Coldfield, Warwickshire, when preparing this illustration and that on the following page.

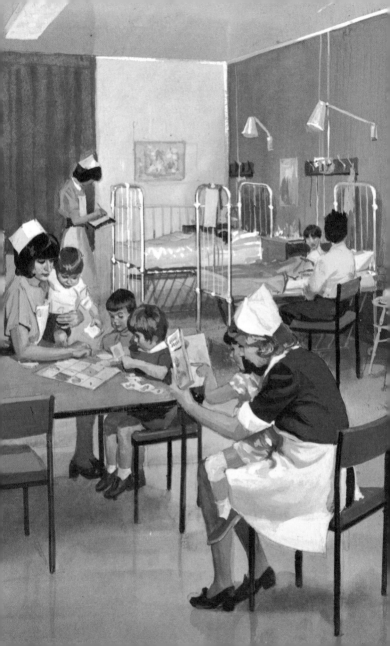

The Hospital Playroom

Some hospitals are fortunate in having a playroom separate from the ward. Here a child who is well enough to be out of bed finds the familiar happy atmosphere of the Playgroup or Nursery School. Mothers and hospital staff are there keeping children happy and occupied. The child who does not want to play finds comfort on the lap of Mother – or of someone else's mother perhaps – or a Nursery Nurse.

The Nursery Nurse is trained to care for the healthy as well as the sick child. She has studied child development and knows the importance of play. Under her guidance the fullest possible use is made of the playroom and its equipment, so that the child can relax in a sympathetic and familiar atmosphere.

There is a book corner, and books with which a child may be familiar, making a link with home. Another link could be the dressing-up clothes and the Wendy house with its dolls, cot, tea-sets and pans. There is possibly an aquarium and a nature table with plants and objects the child recognises. If he wants to paint, to play with clay or water, scissors or paste there is a helpful adult at hand to supervise. The cupboards contain puzzles and games, bricks, crayons and paper. A child who feels well enough will find a tricycle or a pram to push.

In this busy atmosphere the eager child can forget that he or she is in hospital, and the tearful toddler, who is never overlooked, can be helped and comforted.

Discuss the picture with your child.

Playing Shop   'Setting up shop' delights the five-year-olds. It puts them in control of a collection of material of which they know the names, colours, shapes, textures and uses. Children enjoy using their vocabulary to the full in 'sales talk' – in persuasion, argument, and reasoning.

Watching them play in this way, using memory and imagination, we realize just how much a child's learning is being influenced by observation. A child will build into the pattern of play those situations he has seen and conversations he has heard, all very gratifying to parents who have allowed their child time in which to stand and stare, listen and ask questions.

Such things as potatoes, carrots, fruit, etc., are easy to handle and to weigh with kitchen scales. With a little extra care such things as sugar, rice, spaghetti and dried fruit can be weighed and also put into bags. Cartons, bottles and boxes which have contained soap, cosmetics, herbs, coffee, etc., will please by their smell. To a child the world of smells is as new as that of sights and sounds. If we remind ourselves of this from time to time we are more likely to provide the facilities for exploring sights, sounds *and* smells.

Discuss the picture. Encourage questions about the various items, colours, etc.

Glorious Mud   Soil (and *please* call it *soil*, never *dirt*) and water make what to a child is irresistible, glorious mud. So why not use it? It can offer much the same creative possibilities as sand and water, dough or clay.

Why play with mud? Well it is something which costs nothing but with which children can 'cook', make patterns, build, mix into all textures from 'sloppy' to solid, and achieve whatever they wish to achieve to their own great satisfaction, and at the expense of only a little of your patience and tolerance.

Don't be afraid of the wetter, sloshier mixture. Let your child experiment to find out exactly what a wet mixture will and will not do. Let it dry out and crack in the sun – where does the wetness or 'moisture' go? There's a new word – 'moist'. What else is 'moist'?

Remember, children of four or five are conscious of mess and can control it. Please do include mud as useful material in your child's development.

Discuss where mud is usually found – rivers and ponds. Talk about what grows and lives beside and in them – marigolds, ladysmock, frogs, newts, fish, etc. Some marsh birds – thrushes and house-martins – use it to make their nests.

Helping

Allow your children to help around the home – it is a great encouragement to co-operative behaviour. A child's social development begins in its relationship with parents, a development which we must encourage by tolerance of a 'help' or 'assistance' which is perhaps both slow and imperfect.

Children accept that certain routine jobs must be done. They see the consequences of such jobs left undone – for instance, the gloves lost because they were not put away in their correct place, the toy left on the floor and trampled on. They are as unhappy about the consequences as we are.

We need to involve children in our routine, to give them some responsibility and the opportunity to feel satisfaction with their accomplishments. Try to give a child the sort of job that is within his or her capabilities so that satisfaction *can* be achieved. The experience of helping in some useful work, and in learning to follow instructions, is also good preparation for school.

Discuss the picture with your child. Ask your child what are his favourite ways of helping you around the house.

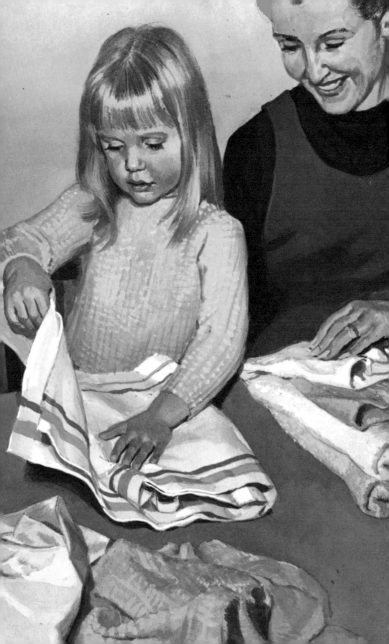

Time for School Starting school is the first major step towards independence in a child's life. The commencing age is usually towards five (although this can vary in some areas), an age when a child is usually sufficiently stable, friendly, obedient and independent enough to carry out small tasks unaided. A mother can help in many ways to prepare a child for school, making sure that all kinds of play materials have been handled and that the company of other children of the same age group has been enjoyed.

Most head teachers invite the next intake of children to visit school during the term previous to their commencement. Mother and child are invited to meet the headmistress and teachers and the visit may be for an hour or for up to half-a-day.

Children are introduced to their new environment and perhaps allowed to wander round other classrooms and see other children at work. They are shown their cloakroom and toilet accommodation and generally made to feel welcome and 'expected'. This visit, prior to starting school, is most valuable to teacher, child and parent and can really reassure an apprehensive child.

Although a child will anticipate school with great pleasure, he or she will panic on occasions, and even after having made a good start will often have a stomach upset, sickness, temperature or be tearful. The best attitude to these temporary setbacks is gentle sympathy and a firm reassurance that it will pass. On no account 'give in' and say "you can stay at home this morning" because this will only prolong what is a comparatively short period of apprehension.

It must be impressed upon a child that once having started, he must go to school every day. It is surprising how many children think that they have only to go for one day, or one week! Make him understand that you will collect him at dinner-time or afternoon home-time, and always be there early – never keep him waiting for this can cause an acute state of anxiety.

Rules in the Infant School, though very few, should be respected – they are made to ensure the smooth running of the school. For instance, do not linger after seeing your child safely into school each day; this only unsettles and upsets him. Tears usually dry up quickly once Mother or Father have gone.

See that your child can dress himself in outdoor clothes and can fasten buttons, shoe buckles and laces, can use a knife, fork and spoon and go to the toilet unaided.

Every article of clothing should be clearly labelled with a child's name in letters *he* can recognise. Shoes, pumps and wellingtons are particularly important. (A small piece of coloured Fablon stuck on each wellington often helps towards easy identification in addition to a name. It is something from home to recognise.) A treasured small toy, which can fit in a pocket or shoebag, is often a comfort in the early days at school.

Lastly, because *you* had one teacher, one classroom and one place to sit in when you were at infant school, do not assume that your child will be in a similar situation. Modern progressive methods of education are such that he or she may have a team of several teachers, several areas

pine cone

nest

bird

tortoise shell

urchin

stick insect

in which to work and play and that the teaching may be co-operative. The headmistress will explain the school organisation to you on your preliminary visit.

Learning today is largely through play situations, so your child is not even aware that he is learning. If possible, refrain from questioning your child about every detail of the day. Your little one is tired physically and mentally at the end of a very active day and may not want to discuss it with you. Little by little you will learn all you want to know by watching and waiting and listening, and through occasional chats with the teacher or teachers. Children often dislike being cross-examined by adults about their world at school.

On this preliminary visit, the child will recognise in many features of school routine, the familiar occupations engaged in at home.

School need not be a completely, strange new world — but rather a development and elaboration of the education begun at home with mother.

Discuss the pictures on this and the previous two pages, how the child and her mother are finding out about the school and are seeing for themselves some of the many interesting activities.

Painting   The child starting school will find that drawing, painting, and modelling are part of the school day. They are essential educational activities which develop eye/hand co-ordination, imagination and the ability to create, as well as being satisfying forms of self-expression second only to the power of speech.

To have had some previous experience of these activities at home, and to have attained some degree of familiarity with the use of the materials, are a great help in adjusting to school life.

Drawing, painting and modelling at school will be a part of home life continued into school, a familiar link with home to give confidence and a sense of security.

Talk to your child. He should by now know all the simple colours by name. Tell him how he can mix them to make other colours – that blue and yellow make green, red and yellow make orange, red and blue make purple – and that a useful brown can be made by mixing everything together!

Puppets

Children love puppets of every kind – whether a quickly improvised one of a paper bag on the hand with a painted face, or a very elaborate one worked with strings or sticks. They love watching them, using them and also making their own. A teacher will often entertain her class with one or two glove puppets and children enjoy bringing their own favourites from home to make up small playlets.

Puppets play a great part in developing speech and communication and a shy child will often speak *through* his puppet, even when too withdrawn to speak for himself.

Sometimes a professional company of puppeteers will visit the school and entertain the children with a performance of a fairy tale, using miniature scenery and tape-recorded sound effects. A short 'follow-up' talk on how to make simple puppets from cereal boxes, match boxes, wooden spoons, paper bags, etc., will encourage interest in the art and craft of puppet making.

Children should be encouraged to use their own ideas to create puppets out of all kinds of scrap materials – boxes, string, ribbon, buttons, papier-mâché and spare scraps of cloth. Sewing is not necessary unless the child wishes, because there are some wonderful adhesives available. The handwork involved in puppet making is valuable in helping a child to be creative and imaginative.

Playing with puppets encourages a child's self-expression and communication with other people.

Discuss the picture with your child.

Making Glove Puppets

These puppets are simple, and with a little supervision can be made by young children.

Materials needed are:

Some pieces of cloth 12″ × 6″; a cardboard egg-box; a toilet roll tube; glue; wool or coarse string; crayons; scissors; a small piece of card.

For the 'girl's' head, a $1\frac{1}{2}$″ length of toilet roll tube should be cut and, after glue has been put on the inside edge, a screwed-up ball of paper should be pushed in (Fig. 1). After glue has been suitably positioned on the paper ball, cut wool can be fixed on as hair (Fig. 2).

The 'girl's' hat (to be put on last) is an egg-box 'cup' pushed into a circle of card, and with a paper ribbon (Fig. 3). A face is painted on the tube.

The 'jerkin' can be made by folding the material in half, forming front and back, cutting a 3″ slot in the middle of the fold for the 'neck', and glueing-up the sides except for the arm holes at the top (Fig. 4). Next, the lower inside edge of the head is glued and the neck of the 'jerkin' pressed inside it, all round; it might be best to stuff this with something until it has stuck fast. The hat should now be put on and fixed with a hat-pin (just an ordinary pin) (Fig. 5).

The 'boy' has a cap made from an egg-box cup cut to shape, with hair made from coarse, teased-out string.

Now put the puppet on your child's hand, with the two middle fingers in the head and an outside finger through each sleeve – and it comes to life!

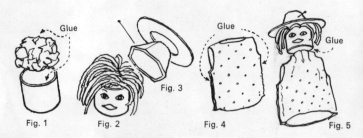

Glue

Fig. 1   Fig. 2

Glue

Fig. 3

Glue

Fig. 4

Glue

Fig. 5

Puppet on a Stick

With your supervision and a little help, your child can make this attractive toy.

Materials needed are:

An empty cream carton; a table tennis ball; wool or fur fabric for the hair; a 12″ piece of dowelling or stick; thin material about 9″ × 5″ for the 'dress'; glue; Sellotape and a little tissue paper or cotton wool.

A small hole should be made in the bottom of the carton and also in the table tennis ball, both holes being large enough to take the stick but at the same time being a tight fit (Fig. 1). Some cotton wool or tissue paper should be pushed into the ball, and then the end of the stick glued and pushed up into it. The stick can then be secured to the head with a 'collar' of Sellotape (Fig. 2).

Glue is then smeared on the top of the ball, and strands of wool (or fur fabric) stuck on for the hair. The face can be drawn with a felt pen. Small buttons make very good eyes (Fig. 3), or these can be scraps of coloured paper cut out and stuck on.

The top inside edge of the carton should be glued and one long edge of the material fixed to it (Fig. 4). The two short edges can then be glued together and left to dry.

When all the glue is dry, the stick should be put down through the dress and carton. The top of the dress is folded around the puppet's 'neck' which is first smeared with glue. A little 'collar' of Sellotape will help to hold it. Two little 'hands' can be cut out and stuck on (Fig. 5).

Your puppet (why not give her a name?) can be made to appear and disappear into the carton as well as turn sideways, by pulling the stick up and down or twisting it from left to right.

Fig. 1   Fig. 2   Fig. 3   Fig. 4   Fig. 5

Glue   Glue   Glue

Pets at Home

After the age of four a child can usually accept a little more responsibility and realise that a pet is *not* just a toy, to be played with for a day or two and then neglected. He can understand its need for continuous routine care, such as he himself has received from his parents.

Most pets call for some degree of adult supervision. Adult help and advice are indicated when cages need cleaning out, when puppies and kittens need toilet training, when hands must be seen to be washed and protective clothing (overalls, etc.) worn. Important, too, is supervision of the pets' diet.

At this age children are avid for information – why there are different breeds of dogs, (for hunting, for herding sheep, as guard dogs, etc.), which food is most suitable, from what is it made and from where it comes and so on. Perhaps they will retain not all of the information offered but enough to make them feel knowledgeable, which is both pleasing and stimulating to them.

Pets have an extending effect emotionally as well as educationally, and while a child's responsibility for his charge cannot always be entire, he is given the opportunity to build into his character, at a formative age, qualities of kindness, understanding, consideration and self-control.

Encourage your child to talk about the picture.

Pets in School

Infant schools encourage the children's interest in pets and there is often a school pet, usually a cat, rabbit, guinea pig or hamster. Fish are popular and interesting, particularly the colourful, tropical ones.

Most important in the reception class is the link with home which can be made by children bringing their own pets to school. Rabbits, guinea pigs, gerbils, hamsters, mice and birds in their cages, terrapins, goldfish in a bowl, all can be brought along provided teacher and parent are willing, and provided the parent can arrange safe transport to and from school. They can stay a whole day or a whole school week. Even puppies and kittens can be brought to school for half a day, or left for an hour or so while mother goes shopping.

Of course there must be a rota, so that the teacher knows which animals are coming to school and can arrange her day accordingly.

Some schools have a 'Pets' Week' or 'Pets' Day' each term, 'Hamster Week', 'Mouse Week', etc. All provide a wonderful link with home, and the most reticent newcomer will feel more at home if able to bring a pet occasionally.

Encourage your child to talk about the picture.

Today
our pets are

John's rabbits

Water Babies

Many primary schools are fortunate in having a swimming pool on the premises. It is usually small and shallow and very suitable for the five year olds' introduction to swimming.

This early approach is carefully planned by the teachers concerned. Mother is also involved, because she is invited to help undress, dry and dress her own and other children, thus forming a home — school link. The timid child *can* stand and watch but this is rarely necessary.

Teacher gives confidence by being in her swim suit in the water. She has a whistle slung on a cord round her neck. This enables her to control the children by quickly attracting their attention.

Children are encouraged to move around the pool, at first holding onto the rail. Then, holding hands, they walk across the pool or, with teacher, form a circle and play 'Ring a ring of roses', 'Here we go round the mulberry bush', 'Looby Loo' — or do the 'Hokey Cokey'.

Splashing is fun and, by holding onto the rail, a child can float his legs to the surface and kick. With all the children doing this together the water becomes a turbulent sea. What fun when teacher swims the length of the pool — it seems the children are trying to sink her.

With floats tucked under their arms they can walk about, perhaps blowing balls across the surface of the water. There is so much action and so much confidence is gained that many children are beginning to swim by their second term in Infant School.

Confidence gained in one field spreads to others, and a child will enthusiastically draw, talk and write about his or her adventures as a water baby.

Christmas Decorations

Here are some Christmas decorations which can be made by your child with a little supervision and guidance.

Materials needed:

Card or stiff paper from cartons or old greetings cards; paint and brush; glue; Sellotape; silver glitter-powder; coloured drinking straws; a milk bottle top and some strong thread.

For the simple flat shapes, the card is folded into two and the two halves glued together except along the fold (where the thread will later be passed). When dry, the shapes – a bell, heart, star, circle or diamond can be cut, (taking care to retain part of the fold at the top), and then painted. A little glue should then be smeared in the centre, or round the edges, or in patterns, and sprinkled with glitter powder. The surplus will shake off leaving the glittering pattern, and the decorations are then ready for threading together.

For the three-dimensional shapes, the cards should be folded and cut as before, but cut out completely so that each is divided into two separate identical shapes – two bells, two stars, etc. Each shape should then be cut along the centre line, the one *down* to half-way, the other *up* to half-way. Each pair of shapes can then be slid together along the cut (Fig. 2) and fixed with a little Sellotape. Thread for hanging can be fixed to them with a little glue or Sellotape. Small lengths of drinking straw can be threaded between the shapes as distance-pieces. They can then be painted and decorated as before.

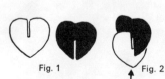

Fig. 1   Fig. 2

The Christmas tree on page 51 is made the same way.

More Christmas Decorations

Materials needed:

Plastic egg-boxes; cardboard egg-boxes; glue; water-colour paint; plastic drinking straws; thread; coloured tissue paper; scissors; milk bottle top; silver glitter-powder.

The cup sections from the egg-boxes can be cut out and shaped like bells. The cardboard ones should be painted, dried, dabbed with glue, perhaps in spots or around the edges, and then sprinkled with silver glitter-powder. The plastic ones should have a little glue inside the cup and a screwed-up piece of coloured tissue paper pushed inside. The outside can be dabbed with glue and sprinkled with glitter-powder. The end of the thread should be knotted and pushed through a screwed-up milk bottle top, then through a piece of drinking straw about 2 inches long, through another bell, another piece of straw and so on until there is a long string of bells to hang on the Christmas tree.

To make the flowers, the cups should be cut out as before, then cut from the edge towards the centre to make the petals, without of course meeting in the middle. The top of the cups then make the flower centres. They can be painted and decorated with glitter.

Christmas Figures from Paper

Materials needed:

Stiff, white paper; white pipe cleaners; glue or Sellotape; water-colour paint and brushes; scissors; a tea plate.

To make the Father Christmas, a circle is drawn (using a tea plate about 8–10 inches across) on stiff, white paper, and cut out. The circle is folded into half and cut across. One half is rolled into a cone shape, (Fig. 1) with a 2 inch overlap which is fixed with glue or Sellotape. The cone should then be painted red.

For the beard, another piece of paper should then be cut about 2½ inches square, folded across and cut out (Fig. 2), opened out and glued onto the cone, about 1½ inches down, by the 'side boards' only. Cut two small slits. The 'moustache' is then cut out, 2 inches wide and fixed with a dab of glue.

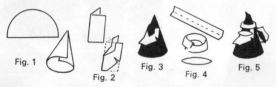

For the hat brim, a piece of paper 1″ by 5″ is folded, the ends tucked together (Fig. 4) and glued in position on the cone. The sack is just a piece of brown paper 2″ by 6″ folded over, screwed-up into a sack and tucked under the hat band with a dab of glue.

For the Angel, a cone is made as before, the wings being cut from the left-over half-circle (leaving enough for the arms), snipped into feathers, pulled under a ruler to curl, and glued on. The arms are in one piece and passed through two slits. The head is a paper circle, stuck on, and the halo is a pipe-cleaner twisted round and stuck in the top of the cone.

Ask your child to find the page from which each picture is taken and talk about what is happening there.

dressing and washing or when helping Mother, he or she is still very dependent on adults for providing opportunities to practise the skills so rapidly being mastered. Vocabulary is still growing rapidly and is still very dependent on the readiness of grown-ups to talk on all topics likely to interest, educate or amuse.

Starting school will present no difficulties to the child who has been encouraged to use his or her initiative and creative capacities during all those days at home with mother. Going to school will be a happy, natural extension into the newer, bigger world.

Also, at this age a child is not too young for an introduction to swimming. Should it not be possible to learn to swim at school, there are many swimming baths with a children's pool which is just right for the supervised beginner and where mother and father can themselves help make the introduction.

This book is intended to help and stimulate all parents who realise the importance of using to the full those situations and materials most likely to develop their child's potential for learning.

adult standards of orderliness, can also 'tidy up' out of existence this priceless potential of intelligence and enterprise, leaving him or her dull and already inhibited at an early age.

This book concerns the child between the age of four and five years, when it develops many new skills, more control over emotions, and closer links with the adult world.

Maybe there are plenty of toys in the home, but do these contribute to your child's development? His toys should be those which are sturdy, simple and adaptable and which encourage both imagination and dexterity.

Complexity is a definite obstruction to imagination. This is why kitchen junk—cartons, plastic bottles, etc.—is so useful. Cartons and bottles will stack and build like bricks; plastic bottles can be cut or shaped for water or sand play or as fitting-together toys—all giving good opportunities for helping your child's development, once you realise the significance of these materials to him. *The subsequent purchase of a really worthwhile toy is then the more easily afforded.*

Although a child in its fifth year shows a great deal of independence, particularly in matters of